CCSS Genre Realistic

Essential Question
How are kids around the world different?

A NEW LIFE IN INDIA

by Christopher Herrera
illustrated by Laura Freeman

CHAPTER 1
Getting to Know India

Mason Jones and his family are moving to India from the U.S. They drive from the airport to their new home. Mason is surrounded by amazing sights. The streets are filled with traffic. Trucks, cars, motorbikes, two-wheeled rickshaws, and bicycles share the road. "I have never seen so much traffic!" Mason exclaims.

Mr. and Mrs. Jones have friends in India. The next day they go to their house. The Guptas have two sons. Raj is in fifth grade. Dev is Mason's age. They will be in second grade together.

Mason is curious to learn more about a special day called School Spirit Day. He can't wait to ask Dev about it.

3

The families go to a cricket match. Cricket is India's favorite sport. Dev and Mason watch the players move around the field.

"Mason, I think you will love cricket! It is similar to baseball. Two teams play each other," Dev explains. "One bats while the other fields. When a player hits a ball, he runs between two areas like bases. These are called wickets. If a person catches the ball, the batter is out. The teams switch places after 10 outs."

After the cricket match, the families have dinner. Mrs. Gupta makes lamb curry. She also makes a spinach and cheese dish, *saag paneer*, and *roti*. *Roti* is a warm, flat bread. Mason likes the food. It is surprisingly spicy. It is filled with different flavors.

roti

saag paneer

paneer

CHAPTER 2

Going to School

The next morning, Mason walks to the Guptas' house. Like Raj and Dev, he wears a white uniform. A driver takes them to their private school.

After their morning classes, Mason and Dev head to the cafeteria and eat sandwiches brought from home. At lunch, Dev describes School Spirit Day.

"I am so excited for School Spirit Day tomorrow! Our class will perform a play. We also get to eat special snacks. At the end of the day, they hand out awards!"

"It sounds fun. I wonder if I will get to be in the play," Mason says.

Mason and Dev have social studies after lunch. They learn about India's independence. It won its independence from Britain on August 15, 1947.

The class shares how they celebrate Independence Day. Dev says, "We go to a parade and get sweets. My family has a picnic. At night, there are fireworks!"

He turns to Mason. "Maybe this year you can celebrate with us!"

Mason tells the class about American Independence Day. "America won its independence from Britain, too. We declared our independence on July 4, 1776. On July 4, Americans celebrate. They have parades. They have picnics, too. At night, there are fireworks. The fireworks are like bright flowers in the sky."

CHAPTER 3

After-school Activities

After school, Mason travels with Dev to Dev's music lesson. Dev is learning to play the tabla, a double drum. Dev shows him how it is played. "I use my fingers and palms. I play one drum with my right hand and one with my left." Dev hands the tabla to Mason. "Here, you try!"

tabla

After tabla practice, the boys go to watch Raj. He is practicing a special Indian dance. It is called *dandyia raas*. Like the other children, Raj wears a fancy, colorful costume. The children form circles that move in different directions. The dancers hold colorful sticks. They hit them together to the beat of the music. They twirl and move their bodies.

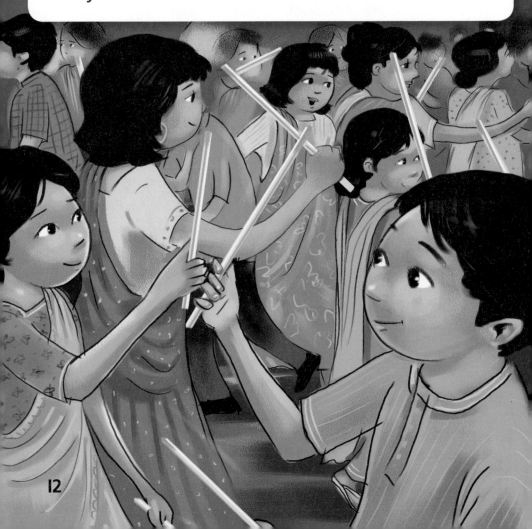

CHAPTER 4
School Spirit Day

School Spirit Day has finally arrived! Everyone is excited. Mason's class will perform a play. Dev and Mason both get parts. They wonder what people will come up with for their costumes.

"I can't wait to perform my lines on stage!" Mason says.

On this day, some children will get awards. Awards will be given to children who do well in their studies. Awards will also be given to those children who do well in sports.

"Maybe we'll both get an award," says Dev. "Wouldn't that be exciting?"

Mason is settling into his new home. He has great friends and a new school. He has already learned so many new customs. "I love it here! I feel like the luckiest kid in the world!" he exclaims.

Summarize

Use important details to summarize *A New Life in India.*

	India	U.S.
holiday		
custom		

Text Evidence

1. How do you know *A New Life in India* is realistic fiction? Genre

2. How are the main characters alike and different? Compare and Contrast

3. Use what you know about similes to find a simile for fireworks on page 10. Similes

4. Write about Mason's new home. Use details to tell what it is like.

   Write About Reading

Ingram Publishing/age fotostock

Compare Texts
What do *A New Life in India* and *Dress Around the World* tell us about customs?

Dress Around the World

In India, some women wear saris. Some women wear them all the time. Others wear them only on special occasions.

A sari is a long strip of cloth. This cloth is wrapped around the body in different styles. It is common to see it draped over the shoulder.

Saris are often printed with colorful patterns.

In Japan, some women and men wear kimonos. They usually wear them for special occasions.

A kimono is a long, square-shaped robe. It is wrapped around the body from left to right. It has a sash called an obi.

Kimonos are often made of silk.

Rich Legg/Vetta/Getty Images

Kanga is a type of clothing worn in eastern Africa. It is worn by women and some men. It is a long piece of colorful printed cloth. It is wrapped around the body in different ways.

The kanga often has a central part with a different design.

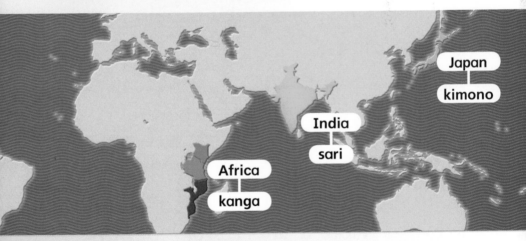

Japan
kimono

India
sari

Africa
kanga

Make Connections

What kinds of clothes might kids around the world wear? Essential Question

Reread both selections. What did you learn about India? Text to Text

Focus on
Literary Elements

Characters Characters are the people in a story.

What to Look for You learn about characters from what they do, where they go, and what happens to them. Look at what the characters say and do in *A New Life in India.* Learn more about Dev and Mason by looking at the illustrations.

Your Turn

Think of two characters living in another country and what they both are like. Plan a short story about these characters. Plan out their actions. Then write your story. Show how your characters are alike and different.